THINKING
BEYOND
CAPITALISM

AN AFRICAN AMERICAN ALTERNATIVE

CYNTHIA HAMILTON

AND

ROBERT TERRELL

Order this book online at www.trafford.com
or email orders@trafford.com

Most Trafford titles are also available at major online book retailers.

Printed in the United States of America.

ISBN: 978-1-4907-3735-5 (sc)
ISBN: 978-1-4907-3737-9 (hc)
ISBN: 978-1-4907-3736-2 (e)

Library of Congress Control Number: 2014909535

Trafford rev. 06/2112014

 www.trafford.com
North America & international
toll-free: 1 888 232 4444 (USA & Canada)
fax: 812 355 4082

Contents

Chapter 1

Thinking Beyond Capitalism

Introduction

What we intend with this book is to encourage thinking about alternatives in the way we live our lives—every aspect, personal and economic. In many areas it's a matter of starting over because some of the mistakes we've made, in our "more is better" philosophy of growth, can't be fixed (for example, environmental problems caused by decisions we've made about farming or weapons production).

While we don't presume to answer the "big" questions we think we can ask them. For example thirty years ago Schumacher declared "small is beautiful"[1]. I don't think there's any doubt that it is but we are afraid to say so if it means we have to choose between big and small. In the U.S. the modern era promised more and better but it hasn't produced that for everyone.

We can look back to antiquity and compare Greece and Rome, clearly problems increased with size but there wasn't complete equality in Greece. We are not attempting to produce a grand new

---

1 E.F. Schumacher, *Small is Beautiful: a study of economics as if people mattered*, 1973

economic theory but the criticisms of capitalism should give us clues about what works and what doesn't even when our intentions are good.

Maybe our discussion will point to goods, the possibility of working with multiple theories/economic systems as long as there is an agreement between countries that colonialism, imperialism, any form of economic or military domination is rejected. Unfortunately, domination is/was an integral part of capitalism as we know it. Capitalism exists because domination was so complete. It was a different form of domination—colonialism—which acknowledged the dominate partner but also recognized the subservient nation as just that. First, as the supplier of workers, second as the supplier of raw materials, third as the consumer of first world produced goods. We can surely see the dependence of the industrial revolution on these relations.

But before we began to consider alternatives (because we must) we have to remember that how we think matters. Capitalism began as a very progressive alternative in the seventeenth century. Feudalism ruled the day, a system which locked you into the condition you were born into. You were either born to survive or not. Economically, you were born into land or not. Money had no meaning. Capitalism developed with slavery, shippers/merchants felt that those who took the risk should be the ones who benefited, not the monarchs. Initially, explorers sailed in the name of the king because he supplied the boats and supplies, the sailors supplied the risk. But when that was not the case the risk-takers wanted all the profits as well.

Initially, what made capitalism so attractive was its democratic side, if you did the work you would be compensated, regardless of family, name, or location. Those who took the risk of exploring a new world could/would be the new owners of land, the new decision makers. Those who took the risk, who worked hard would be the primary actors and beneficiaries. This is what made capitalism seem fair and just (even though there was no regard for indigenous people).

The irony of course is that this is the very component of the system which is absent today.

Capitalism And Slavery:

The Contradictions Are Born

Part of our intention is to explore history to see how capitalism came to be the favored economic system, even though it cannot be separated from domination and oppression.

1492 was the beginning of competition between European countries as we know them, first, for land second for markets. The Pope divided new territories between Spain and Portugal. But, as we know there were many more countries exploring, looking for land and gold. Initially it was the lure of gold but as the Portuguese learned not all land had gold to be mined but that didn't mean there weren't other ways of getting gold from the land. It started with the effort to sell the products of the New World in Europe. But then the issue got more complex—someone had to mine the gold or/and work the land (for the coffee and sugar). There were limits on the number of workers that could be sent from Europe (after all someone had to do the work at home), the native population refused to work. They'd have to bring in workers and then figure out how to get their money back.

When the British moved into Africa it was to follow the trail of gold in the north which the Ghanaians left as they moved east to Egypt in their quest for salt. The gold they found came first from selling products made in Europe. The industrial revolution, slavery, capitalism and the end of feudalism are coterminous. But it is useful to talk about their relationship. Only a few have dared to do this. Eric Williams did in 1944 when he wrote *Capitalism and Slavery*. The book fluctuates in its availability. While there are no absolute reasons why, I can speculate that the major reason is because he documents the necessary relation between the industrial revolution and slavery; slavery provided the financial backing for the industrial revolution. Even banking and insurance originate with the profits from the slave trade. Some of the major industries have their origin with slavery, ship building and weapons production in particular, along with the production of items of trade.

While it is common for people to associate slavery with race and to evaluate it morally/ethically Williams emphasizes that the reasons for slavery are not moral but economic, "they relate not to vice and virtue, but to production."[2] "Slavery was not born of racism: rather, racism was the consequence of slavery. Unfree labor in the New World was brown, white, black, and yellow."[3]

The end of feudalism results almost directly from mercantilism which was built on the slave trade. The bourgeois revolutions, the English (1644), the American (1776), and the French (1789) are a result of this period giving more power to the economic actors at the heart of slavery and the industrial revolution. And finally industrial capitalism destroys slavery. Will it also destroy itself? Slavery and industrial capitalism could not live comfortably together - one side paying workers (though poorly) and the other side owning them. So, finally industrial capitalism destroys slavery but maintains racial hierarchy.

Age Of Enlightenment:

The Contradictions Take Shape

"Individuals and Individualism"

Most of the ideas which shape the way we think come from the period covering the 17th and 18th centuries when the emphasis was on individualism and reason rather than tradition and custom. The irony of the age of Enlightenment is that it is also the age of slavery, the age of contradiction—liberty, equality, and slavery. What allowed Europeans to tolerate this irony is racism.

---

2 Williams, Eric, *Capitalism and Slavery*, Capricorn Books, N.Y., 1944, p. 6.

3 *Ibid., p.7.*

Most of the ideas which shape the way we think fundamentally, come from the age of Enlightenment, when the emphasis was on individualism and reason rather than tradition and custom. The political ideals of the Enlightenment influenced the American Declaration of Independence and the Bill of Rights, the French Declaration of the Rights of Man and Citizen, and Adam Smith's, *Wealth of Nations*. French liberalism and paternalism coupled with ideas about Black inferiority ruled the day. A perfect example is the work of Count Arthur de Gobineau, his four volume work *Essai sur L'Inegalite des Races Humaines (1853-n55)*. He was the first to assert the superiority of the Aryan peoples and among the many to reinforce ideas of black inferiority. The rebuttal to Gobineau came almost immediately from Antenor Firmin in 1885, but was never acknowledged. Only recently has his book become available in translation[4]. Meanwhile de Gobineau's ideas about inequality have influenced all manner of racist thought.

It is ironic that the Enlightenment gave birth to both progressive and reactionary ideas. Political ideas of the Enlightenment influenced the American Declaration of Independence, the French Declaration of the Rights of Man and Citizen, as well as Adam Smith, *Wealth of Nations*, the handbook of capitalism.

The ideas of the Enlightenment informed all of the bourgeois revolutions. The irony of course, is that this was also the era of slavery.

"Endless Growth as Colonialism"

This Age of Reason was also the age of the merchants, and it was their trade and travel which transformed Europe. Not only science, medicine and education generally transformed European cities and society, but the new wealth from trade gave rise to new objectives, "more", became an ideology synonymous with progress.

---

4 Firmin, Antenor, *The Equality of the Human Races*, (translated by Asselin Charles), University of Illinois Press, 2002.nd

Individuals began to feel that more money made them feel secure in challenging the *king's authority*. Taking over more space meant countries could rule like Rome. Slavery was a first step—securing place and then minds.

Capitalism is nothing without expansion—there is always need for more, more markets, more resources, and more workers. *More* itself becomes ideology.

Colonialism and imperialism are built into the system. The consequences of endless growth has resulted in colonialism, both domestic and international, because local markets become saturated and local resources depleted. While people of color and the Third World generally bear few of the fruits of development, they are now asked to be partners in solutions to an environmental crisis created by others. Communities of color in the United States house a disproportionate share of toxic waste. And exporting industrial residues, toxic and radioactive waste to the Third World has become a new form of imperialism.

America's Internal Colony:

Living With Contradictions

"Growth and Blight"

By looking at the Black community as America's internal colony we can really see the contradictions of capitalism—the contradiction between growth and development. It demonstrates that growth and development are simultaneously sources of wealth and improved living conditions as well as death, destruction, and inequality, whether the subject is forests, water, air, or neighborhoods. As Hazel Henderson explains, effective policy is never a matter of growth vs. no growth but rather what is growing, what is declining, and what must be maintained.[5] For people of color, little has been maintained, as communities and neighborhoods decline.

If we take an example, Cabrini-Green Projects (1942,1957, 1962) in Chicago. For years residents complained about conditions and the violence surrounding the projects. When they were rebuilt (in 2010 as townhouses) and rented as mixed income housing we have no idea how many of the original 15,000 residents found new housing. Central city residents who are overburdened with the residue, debris, and decay of industrial production, are not necessarily its beneficiaries. In many cities, growth and development exist beside decay and blighted slums. The two are part of the same process. New development, causing displacement and relocation may be the source of employment for some while eliminating employment permanently for others. The way in which this displacement and inequity occurs is deeply related to injustices long connected with race and class.

It is important, however, to examine issues of urban growth within the broader context of U.S. industrial policy. The imperative to grow or to perish, which dictated the early industrial revolution is no less predominant today. The economic survival of the U.S. rests on this mandate for growth, which has had severe human consequences: environmental destruction, health problems, declining quality of life, and increases in the cost of living. The more we grow, the more resources we use and abuse, the greater the cost of survival. We must begin to ask if growth can occur along with equality rather than greater inequalities. If we cannot grow and develop with constructive rather than destructive production we must consider alternatives to industrial society as we know it.

Whether manifest as the uncontrolled urban sprawl of U.S. cities or the greed that turned rain forests in South America into cattle ranches, development has come to people of color at great cost. In either case, the place that had been home for some

---

5 Hazel Henderson, *The Politics of the Solar Age: Alternatives to Economics* (New York: Doubleday/Anchor, 1981), p. 7.

is appropriated for private use. Inner-city residents have been overburdened with the residue, debris, and decay of the industrial revolution. They bear the burden of growth, soldiering America's waste and its abandoned factories and warehouses. An article in *The Chicago Sun Times* (31 May 1987) described residents of the city's Southside as "victims of environmental neglect that has made the far Southside a mine field of toxic hazards which include abandoned factories, toxic waste dumps, industrial pollution and tainted water."

The real implications of U.S. institutional racism are a result of land-use decisions which ensure that those populations with the most consistent residential proximity to industry in U.S. cities are poor people of color. The central business district of the early twentieth century city was usually the center of the industrial circumference, with people of lower socioeconomic status living closer to the center. African Americans replaced the European ethnic working class completely in this vicinity by the end of World War II. In many instances housing had been built on marshes and garbage dumps. More frequently in the Northeast elevated trains instead of subway tunnels traversed the African American community, with business as usual continuing beneath.

The presence of noise, dirt, rail road tracks, factory pollution, warehouses, and stockyards have become the trademark of African American communities, ensuring de facto segregation. As whites moved away from the inner core of the industrial city to escape its noise, foul air, water, and land, African Americans were allowed to move into the houses left behind. This has made the boundaries of African American communities' natural divisions such as rivers or lakes or major highways, on whose banks we are sure to find factories, warehouses and stockyards.

Only after the organized union drive of the 1930's did industry discover the advantages of relocating to the urban periphery or finding new locations in the Sunbelt or later in the Third World, taking advantage of cheap land and labor, moving away from the industrial Northeast. Class relations shaped the urban landscape and the emergent conflict that characterized the new urban industrial cities. The power of workers was enhanced by the concentration in large numbers and the centralized nature of product ion. The historical transformation in the structure of cities has been propelled not by technological development alone but by the need to reproduce existing class relations in the capital accumulation process. To escape workers' demands, industries began to move away from cities' urban core into the suburbs, aided by government subsidies for industries producing for the war effort. Public housing and highway legislation facilitated the transit of workers and commodities. The desertion of the inner city left a decaying core. Dispersing workers inhibited their capacity to organize effectively.

"Environmental Destruction and Capitalism"

The decay of the inner city has become common. This is an internationally recognized condition, as indicated by the World Commission of Environment and Development. They wrote:

"Industrial cities account for a high share of the world's resource use, energy consumption, and environmental pollution . . . Many industrial cities face problems of deteriorating infrastructure, environmental degradation, inner city decay, and neighborhood collapse. The unemployed, the elderly and racial and ethnic minorities can remain trapped in a downward spiral of degradation and poverty as job opportunities and younger and better educated individuals leave declining neighborhoods. City or municipal governments often face a legacy of poorly designed and maintained public housing estates, mounting costs, and declining tax bases."[6]

The report also notes that the resources exist to solve the urban-environmental crisis in industrial countries and therefore "the issue for these countries, is ultimately one of political and social choice."[7] In most instances the choice has been to build a

---

6 World Commission on Environment and Development, *Our Common Future,* (New York: Oxford University Press, 1987). 24.

7 Ibid. 25

new urban core, to displace the poor and create a new corporate city to serve a new set of functions. Cities are needed not to centralize production but rather to house administrative and financial headquarters such as bank, stock exchanges and insurance companies. The reorganization of capital and the need to maintain control of workers facilitated urban restructuring. A new corporate form replaces the old industrial city, not only in appearance but with new inhabitants, displacing the poor and working class. Decentralization and sprawl (aided by technology) have replaced centralization. This new form has also displaced a major source of social justice that communities have historically provided for their resident. Left to their own devices, poor communities in the 1930's and 1960's organized to fill gaps in services left unprovided for by local government. Communities not only provided a sense of cultural identity for residents but also offered an antidote for alienation, loneliness, and racial harassment. They offered safety and security to residents. Historically, communities provided their own safety nets through self-help organizations. For example, they organized funds of injured workers and widows; neighbors banded together to collect money for rent or came together to resist eviction. As late as the 1960's, African American communities recognized community control as a self-help strategy. The collapse of community has left residents completely dependent on government service and subject to the consequences of urban restructuring.

But the loss of community was no accident. Much like the movement of industry to the periphery of cities, the 1940's and 1950's which dispersed workers as they moved to the new suburbs following jobs, African American communities have been dispersed. Suburbanization is an instrument of dispersal, but new development at the city's center has also displaced and dispersed African Americans. Without community, African Americans have lost an important center of cultural and political identity that could offer an alternative source of affirmation and resistance. After 1965 and the passage of the Voting Rights Act, urban concentration also proved being a political asset as African Americans elected representatives in urban areas. Without community, this type of action is impossible.

Uneven development and change have shaped power relations between nations and individuals over the past three centuries. We have known these relations by different names: colonialism; imperialism; underdevelopment; racism; or internal colonialism. This is a result of the centuries of uneven development and exchange and the century of intense industrial production. The most advanced stage of industrialization has been the most toxic. Resulting from the minimally controlled petrochemicals, electronics, and aerospace industries.

Developments' horrors in communities of color are rampant. Children farm workers suffer birth defects as a consequence of their mothers' pesticide exposure at work during pregnancy. In and around farm worker communities, child cancer rates are high. Children whose mothers have worked in the high tech industries, where the use of dangerous chemicals is common, have high rates of birth defects. Children living around military installations have higher rates of cancer and other illnesses.

To halt this self-destructive march of industrial growth and development requires citizen action guided by a critical approach to community development and industrial production. Such action must transcend isolated, individual crises and attempt to confront the natural consequences of corporate, industrial behavior. So far, environmental activists and thinkers have been slow to develop a theory of political action or community development because of the focus on instrumentalities: rules; bureaucracy and administration (in the tradition of liberal and conservative thought). What is needed is an economic democracy that must include, first an end to macroeconomic approaches to planning and assessment and the institutionalization of decentralization, local and regional approaches to development. Cities have begun the center of injustice as a result of current development models; alternatives should be conscious of the multiple needs at this level. New planning must be undertaken in cities incorporating neighborhood voices. Second, we must focus our attention on renewable resource methods (e.g. solar energy and recycling) over nuclear energy.

Third, our political assessment and approach within a new framework of an ecology of democracy must recognize class interests in Western and developing societies. Alternatives require us to acknowledge the political intentions and consequence of growth and development strategies, intentions that include the destruction of working class communities in the inner city. This approach necessitates rejecting an assessment of development as simply a technological advance and thereby politically neutral.

Fourth, a new social contract is necessary between citizens and the State as well as between citizens and representatives and participatory forms. Corporations have used special interests processes to influence political officials and thereby government decisions. Consequently, present political leadership is completely unresponsive to communities. Before accountability can be assured, new leadership and new forms of participation will be necessary; multiple decision making units, such as neighborhood councils, are needed to regulate development and insure citizen input on growth decisions. Centralized units of political decision making as well as centralized planning methods must be replaced by decentralized units. This is the essence of what Hazel Henderson means by "thinking globally and acting locally."8

The challenge feared most by the corporate sector is one that substitutes the collective good for their much promoted philosophy of individualism. When groups previously left out of formal parliamentary and electoral processes demand access or develop new methods of political action, capitalists feel threatened. Struggles of urban African Americans in cities against the consequences of unbridled growth have much to contribute to the new environmental movement. For African Americans in the legally segregated "separate but equal" society, the personal commitment to change is reflective of social concerns. Demanding broad social change was a prerequisite for expanded personal

---

8 Henderson, *Politics of the Solar Age, p.355*

rights and freedoms. Unfortunately, industrial society forced the separation of private and social concerns. As a result, individuals are locked into selfishly considering individual rights rather than cooperating to meet community needs.

The essence of a new social contract must therefore be the reaffirmation of the common good. Livable cities will only be possible when the collective good is understood to have meaning for each individual. Community agenda must replace the current corporate agenda for American cities, so that we would be forced to consider issues of sustainability: employment; livable space; resource management that avoids excessive waste and pollution control as a health measure. But this community agenda would also revive a notion of the collective good; social concerns would become more central than private good. Individuals and collective good can no longer remain separate. The false contradiction between social good and individual rights and needs has produced the current problems and crises. This community agenda must therefore be prefaced by a new social contract that reaffirms the common good. Individual property rights must no longer be permitted to infringe on the quality of life effecting everyone.

Chapter 2

An African American Alternative

Our primary concern is that Black communities, poor communities generally, while serving as the unacknowledged workhorse of American industrial development, these communities are dead. Black and poor families are left alone, struggling to survive. There is no collective defense against racism, no shared resources when individual resources have disappeared, no informal learning of skills needed for survival. Without community even the capacity to resist disappears; there is no longer the organizing which community supplied. Without community even the capacity to resist disappears, there is no longer the organizing which community supplied. Without community we must consider the alternatives which are described in the following part of this book.

Introduction

It is our intention that this policy memo serve several functions; (i) present ideas on how best to revitalize African-American communities, (ii) provide a foundation for public policy statements and (iii) serve as a guide for future research. Secondarily, this memo is intended to serve as a statement to the larger African-American community as to the seriousness of the current crisis we face and the alternatives that exist to resolve it. It is our hope to contribute to the building of a new social movement that will empower African-Americans, revitalize our communities and contribute to building a just society.

W.E.B. DuBois wrote in the 1920's that" the problem of the 20th century will be the problem of the color line" (1). Racism and discriminatory behavior have been key aspects of American society from its inception and continue to exist in many parts of American life. The Civil Rights/Black Power movements of the 1960's and 1970's did secure some measure of political rights and legal protections with the passage of the 1964 and 1968 Civil Rights Acts and the 1965 Voting Rights Act. Even with the attacks upon civil rights laws by conservative political forces, (e.g. the defeat of the ERA, the Bakke Decision, the Crosen Decision, the Sandoval Decision, etc.), African-Americans have continued to break down some racial barriers.

All the recent demographic and socio-economic data from the 2010 U.S. Census and other sources show that the majority of African-Americans still have a long way to go in gaining complete parity and equality with white, mainstream America. Whether we examine data on home ownership, college graduation, high school drop-outs, income, employment, health care or other key variables, African-Americans continue to lag behind their white counterparts and in some areas, such as education, the gaps are widening (2). While the standard of "being equal to whites" as a social and economic goal is in and of itself highly problematic and needs to be challenged, the picture created by the current demographic profile makes two things very clear. African-American communities continue to suffer from high levels of poverty, underdevelopment and dependency and are internal colonies of the larger American economy. This view was first expressed by Dr. Kenneth Clark in 1960 in his sociological study, *Dark Ghetto* (3). Since then a number of scholars and theorists, such as Harold Cruse, Robert L. Allen, Robert Blauner, John Bracey and others have further elaborated on the internal colony thesis which I believe best describes the conditions that persist in African-American communities. In another forthcoming study for the 21st Century

Institute I will provide up-to-date empirical data from the 2012 Economic Census to further substantiate this view.

However, much has changed in America since the high point of the Civil Rights movement that has significantly shifted the political terrain and the economic environment. In fact there have been five major changes in the last 40 years that need to be acknowledged. **First** has been the emergence of other interest groups; women, gays, Latinos, Asians, Native Americans, migrant workers, immigrants, etc. who share the civil rights agenda. **Second**, with Earth Day in 1970 and the passage of the Clean Water and Clean Air Acts of 1972, the modern Environmental Movement arrived on the scene and began to challenge every school of economic thought (free market, Keynesian, Marxian, etc.) as to their belief in permanent economic growth in a world of limited resources. **Third**, in 1973, America was hit by its first major energy crisis (partly due to an Arab oil embargo by OPEC in response to the 1973 Yum Kipper War and a second oil shock in 1977) as if to underscore many of the warnings made by the Environmental Movement. This energy crisis signaled the end of total, low-cost, energy abundance and put the issue of energy-efficiency, conservation and sustainable development permanently on our national agenda. **Fourth**, between 1970 and 1990 America became slowly and painfully aware of the increasing amount of economic competition and integration on an international scale. Globalization had arrived and the five recessions suffered by the United States in this period only served to prove that America's economic fate was no longer in its hands alone. **Fifth**, was the technological boom since 1980—the Information Revolution—that changed the United States from an industrial to an informational economy. The revolution in computer technology, telecommunications, the rise of the Internet and the massive use of electronic miniaturization has changed almost every occupation, profession and industry and placed an increasing emphasis on scientific, technical and mathematical skills.

What this means in simple terms is that the America confronted by the Civil Rights movement has been changed. The political and economic terrain of American society has shifted in some dramatic ways. Just as Dr. Ralph Bunche wrote his famous essay, "Ideology, Organization, Strategy and Tactics of Negro Improvement Organizations" in 1937 as an attempt to reassess the effectiveness of the Black movement during the Great Depression, so we must do the same today in light of the monumental changes that have come about over the last 40 years.

The 21st Century Institute believes that as African-Americans enter the second decade of the new millennium we must take a new and fresh approach to the problems that confront us. We believe that the revitalization of our communities and the restoration of our culture will rest upon the promotion and exercise of four essential principles; economic democracy, political empowerment, sustainable development and applied mathematics and science. It is to these principles that I now turn.

Economic Democracy

The total assets of the U.S. economy amount to $180 trillion, yet less than1% of these assets are owned by African-Americans (4). This is all the more frustrating when we realize that African-Americans spend $630 billion per year as consumers (5). This is a level of consumption greater than the total GDP of most nations and would rank us the 19th largest economy in the world (6). From these two economic indicators alone it is clear what must be done. The African-American community must undertake an aggressive policy of entrepreneurship designed not only to increase our percentage of business ownership but to reclaim the business network within our own communities. With the massive changes taking place in the U.S. economy and the emergence of entirely new sectors, African-Americans must be prepared to participate as owners, investors, managers and employees.

However in the formation of these new businesses and economic enterprises, we must ask if the conventional methods of business organization and operation are in concert with the needs of our communities. If we hope to successfully address the issues of poverty, economic inequality, underdevelopment and dependency; then we must be willing to examine a host of new policies and programs. These policies and programs are designed to bring about a democratic pattern of ownership, inclusive decision-making and a more humane distribution of wealth and income. To this end Charles Hubert Hammond, has developed what he calls, "The Seven Pillars of Economic Democracy". These are seven essential building blocks that if pursued will develop an economy that spreads prosperity and stability throughout our community and serve as a model for the larger society as well.

Cooperatives

The first "pillar" is that of consumer cooperatives. While many progressive and radical economic theories strictly focus on workers and workplace politics, we often forget that people have another kind of power. Not only can they withhold their labor-power as workers but they can withhold or redirect their purchasing power as consumers. Currently some 800 million people worldwide participate in cooperatives (7). By collectivizing their purchasing power within a consumer cooperative and focusing their spending on certain companies, consumers can obtain significant discounts in prices. For example, the majority of people within the African-American community have low incomes and food has become more expensive. A food cooperative could be organized that would allow people to buy all or most of their food from one source; retail, wholesale or directly from farmers (8). The sellers will lower their per unit prices to receive such a large amount of business over a specified period of time which could be agreed to in a contract. The sellers will make back in volume what they give up in price. This could also provide rural farmers what they have always needed to get out from under the monopoly of large agri-business companies: direct access to an urban market that provides them consistent and larger incomes. Agri-business companies generally pay farmers far less for their product then what it sells for by the time its reaches the supermarket (9). If farmers had direct access to African-American consumers, who agreed to buy their products directly, they would increase their profit margins and the consumers would save a significant amount of money.

Building a network of consumer cooperatives throughout the African-American community would allow help people to buy clothing, appliances, new energy technologies, home improvements, or medical care at reduced costs (10). These cooperatives can be organized by anyone; a group of interested residents, a neighborhood association, tenant group or religious institution. The larger a cooperative grows in membership, the higher the discount it will be able to leverage. As cooperatives gain more members and economic strength they may decide to impose an internal surcharge, accumulate a surplus and hire their own members or local residents to handle certain administrative tasks. In this way cooperatives can become a source of jobs.

It has been pointed out that 75% of the inflation in our economy is centered on food, housing, clothing and medical costs (11). If we save the African-American community just a mere 10% on its consumer spending in these four areas the overall impact would be substantial and while housing costs would be more difficult to reduce, it has been documented that other areas of consumer spending could be reduced by as much as 30%. Depending on how people decide to utilize their additional income (save, consume or invest) this strategy could result in several economic benefits; an increase in disposable income, potentially a higher rate of savings, additional capital for investments, less consumer borrowing, lower interest rates due to the decline in the demand for credit and increased local employment.

Unions

However, let's not forget about the workers all together. If we hope to see any improvement in the unequal distribution of wealth and income in African-American communities, then workers, regardless of occupation, trade or industry, whether urban or rural, must have the right to organize and negotiate for decent wages, conditions and benefits. Just after World War II, as a result of the CIO union drives in the 1930's, 35% of the American workforce was in unions and wages, to some extent, keep pace with inflation and profits until the late 1960's (12). Today, we have seen a massive erosion of real wages for American workers in the 1995-2007 period (before the Great Recession) even as the economy, productivity and profits grew (13). This erosion is directly related to the decline of the American Labor Movement which has occurred for several reasons; a concerted strategy of union-busting by conservative political and corporate forces, the sabotaging of union-certification elections, illegal actions against union organizers, the pursuit of right-to-work laws designed to keep unions out of various states, the lack of unionization amongst white collar workers, forced "give-backs" during contract negotiations, the decline of U.S. manufacturing, the lack of interest in or knowledge about unions by young people and the impact of globalization on the mobility of capital. Add to this the traditional hostility of some unions to admit workers of color and women and it's quite understandable why the power of unions has declined. In fact only 12% of the American workforce is in unions today (14).

Many of the gains made by African-Americans in the 1960's and 1970's were due to their entry into occupations that were unionized and they began to see their wages and benefits improve (15).With the coming of deindustrialization and the decline of unions starting in the 1980's, African-Americans saw many of these gains wiped out (16). In fact we witnessed a major decline in the African-American working class itself as a major social component of the Black community (17). We believe that a re-birth of the labor movement through education and grassroots organizing is not only key to the development of economic democracy but an essential ingredient in the economic revitalization of African-American communities. Black workers, as they have done in the past, must play a leading role in a new, revitalized labor movement that will benefit all workers in the United States and help create the conditions for economic democracy within Black communities (18).

Employee Stock Ownership Programs (ESOP's)

However we should not look at workers as employees alone. They are the producers of wealth as well, contributing their "value-added" to every product through both their physical labor and intellectual creativity (19). As such the owners and investors of any firm cannot be seen as the sole source of all creativity, ingenuity or innovation and therefore cannot lay sole claim to a company's profits or net worth. The concept of private property and ownership may be a virtue but it does have its limitations (20). All economic enterprises within our community utilize some kind of profit-sharing system. ESOPs are usually found in medium and large-scale firms and are found in a large number of U.S. companies today (21). ESOPs would allow the workers to share in the ownership of the company through the purchasing of shares of stock. As shareholders they are not only entitled to a share of the profits through dividend payments but can attend stockholder meetings, compete for seats on the board of directors and have access to information about the firm. This, along with union representation, would be another mechanism for bringing about a better distribution of wealth and income and keep more wealth within our communities.

Consumer Stock Ownership Programs (COSOPs)

However, the same way companies can impact workers, consumers and investors, they can affect communities as well. Not only do companies provide direct employment but they have secondary and tertiary connections as well. They might need local resources for maintenance, security, accounting, legal counsel, banking services and basic supplies. For this reason when a company, particularly a major employer, locates to another region or moves overseas it can have devastating results for the local population. COSOPs would allow members of the community to invest in the company and have local capital play a role in development projects (22). Combined with possible investments from workers (ESOPs), local business interests and the government (local, state or federal), no company will be able to dominate the situation. If a company choose to leave the area there would be many partners to deal with and transparency will be demanded. Even if they do leave, people from the community will still have their investment in the company and could continue to derive some benefit from the operation of the firm. If sophisticated investors can do so, why not workers and community residents?

Land Trusts

Land is crucial to our discussion because all development takes place on land. Oftentimes when development is discussed it is left out of the equation. In a development project land can be either bought or leased. Most developers do not have a preference as long as the numbers do not hurt their bottom line and fit the projections within their pro forma. However, land is a very valuable asset to any community. The community could organize a local land trust that would be controlled by a group of local residents. The land trust would hold the land and collect a ground-rent from the entity leasing it. The land trust could use the money collected to buy and preserve more land or reinvest it back into the community. In this way African-American communities would begin to build up their own source of capital for local needs and use its ownership of land to influence the course of future development (23).

Community Development Corporations (CDCs)

CDCs are very popular in urban areas and African-American communities throughout the United States. While the jury is still out on their overall effectiveness I believe they do have some potential. Despite their inherent strengths and weaknesses the basic theory behind CDCs is sound. Local residents form a CDC and by controlling its governance structure, make decisions on what types of development to pursue. As long as it remains open to all residents within the specified community and the decision-making process is democratic, CDCs can have a positive impact. If successful they will begin to accumulate capital of their own or be able to attract additional investors and partners. As such they can become another independent source of local capital that insures participation and control by local residents in the future development of African-American communities (24). Many CDC's specialize in commercial and business development which can be a major vehicle for bringing new jobs into the African-American community.

Credit Unions

Once a community begins to increase its earnings, save money due to the lowering of prices, develop local entrepreneurship and derive the benefit of its investments, the question emerges on how best to get the maximum benefit from all this activity. One way is to pool these funds in a financial intermediary (bank) so that there will be not only a place to store one's funds but a source of loans and credit. No matter how successful, there will be times when entities will not be able to finance their needs from their own cash flows and will require some form of debt or equity financing. However, banks and major lending institutions have historically not been helpful to African-American communities (25). Given their legacy of redlining, predatory lending and foreclosures why should our communities continue to do business with these institutions. African—American communities should organize credit unions or cooperatively-owned banks that would be controlled by local residents. They would set the rules and standards for lending, lend to local people and projects and by circulating their capital locally avoid the interference of outside institutions. By creating local economic linkages and keeping more of the money within our communities we will receive the benefits of the economic "multiplier effect" where we maximize the impact of our dollars by increasing their circulation within our community.

These seven pillars of economic democracy are just the first steps that can be taken to revitalize African-American communities and liberate them from the legacy of poverty, unemployment, underdevelopment and dependency. Only by developing a vibrant, mixed economy composed of for-profit, non-profit and cooperative enterprises will the African-American community be able to overcome these challenges.

Housing and The Non-Speculative Market

The foreclosure crisis of 2008 forced everyone to reconsider the way in which we finance housing; we had experienced a similar crisis in 1986 with Savings and Loan institutions. But, now banks were the culprit. It wasn't simply the way we financed housing but also the way in which we established price. We know that exchange values rain supreme and use value is ignored in a market economy but when housing is the product being considered, everyone should worry. Not only is housing a basic need, the things that raise the value of housing is different for families then for banks/Wall Street. Prices continue to go up, irrespective of jobs, income, family size and other tangible phenomenon.

As more and more families loss their housing with fewer and fewer ways of retrieving it, it is clear that all Americans must begin to reimagine housing. We must learn to emphasize use and remove housing from the arena of exchange value alone. The problems continue as we now see cash replacing financing as a means of purchase.

More and more homelessness threatens the most developed country in the Western world.

Political Empowerment

As African-Americans know from our history, economic gains must be protected by political power and institutionalized by legal procedure. Some of the greatest political debates in African-American history have centered around this very question;

Frederick Douglass and Martin Delaney over the abolition of slavery, W.E.B. DuBois and Booker T. Washington over anti-segregation strategy and Malcolm X and Martin Luther King over civil rights strategy. Therefore, it is essential that African-Americans increase their participation at all levels of American politics. Yet, how we do so needs to be seriously reexamined. We must question the role of political parties, elections, legislative bodies, the courts and their ability to bring about a democratic and truly representative system. The African-American community must decide how it wants to engage the system and with what agenda. Currently there is a serious debate about how to change the U.S. political system and the African-American community must be a part of this debate to determine which set of political arrangements affords us the best opportunity to pursue our interests. Even at the level of conventional, electoral politics, Black candidates find themselves at a disadvantage because they are not utilizing the latest technologies and techniques for fundraising, voter ID, GOTV operations, or targeted field operations. A great deal of political education for candidates and voters alike still needs to be done, just to improve access to the current system.

In addition to electoral politics, we need to strengthen our political activities outside of government. Community-based and workplace organizing is still essential for impacting public policy. However, political movements must be far more sophisticated in the 21st century if they are to be successful and need to have a higher degree of technical expertise. Real empowerment comes when people have a chance to speak, plan and act on their own behalf and we must be aware of any opportunity to decentralize the political structure and place real decision-making power in the hands of people.

Proportional Representation

One of the major problems with the current political system is that elections are decided on a winner-take-all basis. If a candidate wins an election with just 51 % of the vote, they win the seat.

But what happens to the 49% of the electorate that did not vote for them? They are essentially without representation. It is this winner-take-all method that has made it difficult for third parties to have any real impact, resulting in a virtual monopoly over American politics by the Democratic and Republican parties (26). Also the idea of one person being able to represent an entire geographical district is a quaint 18th century idea that has become dis-functional. In the 18th century when white, male, property-owners simply represented others of their class, the system worked reasonably well. But today many kinds of people participate in the process with a myriad of views and interests. This has created an environment of political dissensus, that is the absence of any real political consensus (27). Without such a consensus, who and what does the elected official represent? More often than not the elected official will fall prey to either the best financed or best organized elements within their district. This state of affairs is not any better in African-American communities where political empowerment is greatly needed.

Through the reform of our election laws we need to shift to a system of proportional representation. Under this system a political party is awarded the number of seats in a legislative body commensurate with the percentage of votes it receives in the election. If a party receives 20% of the vote then it gets 20% of the seats in a legislative body. This would allow all political parties to participate, break the two-party monopoly, provide all voters some level of representation and guarantee that groups of citizens can organize around a narrowly or broadly defined set of interests. Provisions can also be made for people who prefer to run as individuals and not part of any political party.

This would be very advantageous to the African-American community. African-Americans could vote as an electoral block (bullet voting) or develop electoral coalitions to expand their influence. Either way it would guarantee a higher level of representation depending on how our votes are deployed. This flexibility could be used to tailor our political strategy to local conditions, maximize our political power and have more influence on public policy.

One Man, Many Votes?

The act of voting itself has oftentimes been a barrier and African-Americans need to support reforms that make it easier for people to vote. First we need to end voter registration. This was initially put in place as a method for cleaning up the voter fraud and corruption of big-city political machines which were viewed by urban elites as a mechanism for empowering working class people (28). Voter registration has been the means by which many are discouraged from voting and to keep voter turnouts low. People should not been required to register but simply identify themselves using their birth certificate, social security card, baptismal record or any document that's shows they are a citizen of the United States.

Second, Election Day should be a holiday perhaps extended for two or three days to allow people the maximum amount of time to vote. Third, a person should be allowed to cast more than one vote. One vote for one candidate or political party is not sufficient to reflect all of a person's interests. Assuming we have changed to a system of proportional representation and have various parties to choose from, a person should be allowed to cast 10 votes. For example, 3 votes for a labor party to reflect their class interests, 3 votes for an ethnic party to reflect their racial/ethnic identity and 3 votes for a gender-based party and perhaps 1 vote for an environmental party. Such a system would more accurately reflect the political will of the voting public and prioritize the issues to be addressed by a legislative body.

These reforms would help the African-American community expand its voter base, increase its voter participation, assert its political influence in all areas of public policy and place it in a much better position to protect its interests.

Public Financing of Elections

A key reform that would help to make our political system more democratic would be the public financing of political campaigns. This would level the playing field between all candidates and parties if we allocated the same amount of funds to each contestant and gave them the same amount of access to the press and media. As new political parties, perhaps those emerging from the African-American community, come into the process they will be guaranteed the same level of resources as older, more established parties.

Decentralization of Government

If democracy is going to expand African-Americans must advocate for a series of policies that would begin to decentralize the power of the State. The executive branch of government has a monopoly on the implementation of government policies but we must advocate for new forms of direct, participatory democracy that places decision-making power and responsibility for implementation in the hands of people. An excellent place to begin would be issues such as; community development, education, public health, housing and transportation; the results of which would have direct impact on people's daily lives. Advisory committees, civic engagement or solicitation of people's "input" is not enough. Real power through community councils, regional bodies, worker-owned cooperatives and other types of direct democracy, must be conferred on people as an actual requirement of progressive legislation.

Coordination of parliamentary and extra-parliamentary politics

A key weakness of progressive movements throughout the course of American history has been their lack of coordination between their parliamentary and extra-parliamentary politics. If the political empowerment of the African-American community is to take place then we must find better ways of connecting our community/workplace organizing to our political activities inside government. If we do not, then our grassroots movements will be cut off from major centers of decision-making and our elected/ appointed officials will become isolated within the bureaucracy of the State.

Sustainable Development

As mentioned earlier, the Environmental Movement has placed several challenges before all schools of economic thought by advocating for the reduction of air, water and soil pollution, conservation of fossil fuels, conversion to renewable energy resources, increasing the energy efficiency of all industries but most important of all challenging the traditional notions about economic growth and expansion. It has been made clear that our current mode of growth based on the industrial model of the 18th and 19th centuries simply cannot be sustained in a world of finite resources (29). Therefore we need a model of development that is sustainable and capable of functioning within the limits of our environment.

With its emphasis on energy-efficiency, the environmental movement stressed the need for technologies of appropriate size and scale (30). This is highly important to communities that do not have the large amounts of capital required for traditional industrial development. Today it is possible to foster new forms of development at a lower cost and with less impact on the environment. Thus, sustainability and the underlying concepts of ecology and entropy have changed the way we view economic development and must be at the center of any discussion about the future revitalization of African-American communities (31). We must also be aware that the demand for a cleaner, more energy-efficient system has opened up new business opportunities and areas of employment. The "greening" of the American economy is still in its infancy and now is the time for African-Americans to get in on the ground floor.

Land Use and Environmental Racism

All too often, land in African-American communities is used as a dumping ground for waste disposal or the placement of toxic industries. In fact 75%-80% of all such activities are sited in communities of color nation-wide (32). To prevent this from occurring the following steps should be taken to gain more land use control within our communities.

- The establishment of neighborhood councils by local residents to implement community-control of development and monitor all zoning, urban design, capital improvement and land use policies.
- The development of a community-wide set of economic, environmental and employment standards that will make it clear to anyone wishing to develop in our community what our standards are and that we intend to enforce them.
- The banning all toxic industries such as chemical plants, landfills, incinerators, nuclear power plants and asphalt plants from our communities.
- The organization of community-based land trusts to hold strategic parcels of land until we find the resources or interested parties to develop them according to our wishes. Land trusts have been used throughout the U.S. to preserve park lands, open space, historic buildings and promote affordable housing.
- Each of our communities should develop a master plan that clearly designates what land is available for development, what it is zoned for and its final use. Such a plan will serve as a public policy document to guide our future land use and control the outcomes of any new investment.

Energy Efficiency

It is highly important that we take seriously an idea that has shaped a great deal of environmental politics over the past 30 years. That idea is expressed by the slogan, "think globally but act locally". This means that our greatest contribution to stopping the wholesale destruction of our planet rests on how we behave in our everyday lives. Residential (especially affordable housing), commercial, retail and industrial development are serious long-term goals within the African-American community but to make them a reality, the issue of energy and utility costs must be addressed. It is estimated that 20 to 30 percent of real estate costs are energy/utility-related (water, heating oil, gas, electricity) (33). In the near future the cost of these energy resources will rise as their intense depletion continues. We must immediately begin a gradual process of shifting our energy use to renewable resources that can be utilized without any kind of pollution (34). As part of its overall development standards, the African-American community must implement a research program to determine how renewable energy technologies can be applied to all kinds of buildings and structures. A goal should be set to retrofit as many buildings and economic enterprises as possible with the objective of significantly reducing pollution, decreasing energy use and saving money through the reduction of costs. Such a strategy will be vital to the future success of any economic enterprise and is absolutely essential if we hope to build and sustain affordable housing in the future. Such renewable or energy-saving technologies include:

- active and passive solar energy, hydrogen fuel cells, wind turbines and tidal turbines for the production of electricity
- low-wattage appliances that use less electricity
- low-flow water devices for kitchens and bathrooms that utilize less water
- insulation that lowers the cost of heating and cooling a building

Food and Urban Agriculture

Food has a major impact on our health and our continuing development. Often our community finds itself spending far too much for food that is of poor quality. Because of our income levels, we sometimes buy cheaper cuts of meat or highly processed food that use large amounts of chemical preservatives, sugar, salt and fat. We need a serious environmental policy that stresses neighborhood food security and the elimination of "food deserts" within our community. A comprehensive food security network would include;

- Food cooperatives owned and operated by local residents or organized through neighborhood associations, tenant groups, churches or CDC's. Cooperative could operate on either a small-scale for a hundred households or on a large-scale like a supermarket.
- Small grocery stores throughout the neighborhood that come together and purchase their food from a common wholesaler. This would reduce their costs and the prices they would need to charge, saving money for local residents.
- Utilization of vacant lots for urban agriculture. A lot could be shared by local residents with each person growing vegetables or fruits of their choice. Other lots could be used to grow food for local grocery stores, supermarkets, restaurants or sold at farmer's markets. Because it is locally grown its price will be lower providing additional savings to residents.
- Either through cooperative purchases or local growing we can encourage the use of organic farming methods that will provide us with healthier, more nutritious food.
- Our community can be very helpful to farmers in this regard if we seriously pursue a recycling policy. This would not only return various materials to manufacturers for reuse but recycle our organic waste into compost piles that could be sold to farmers. This would provide local residents

with jobs and farmers with a source of organic, rather than chemical, fertilizer.

- Through our food cooperatives, we could buy some of our food directly from local farmers (individually or through farmers' markets) and receive a major discount in return for buying a substantial percentage of their crop. The African-American community could spend less money on food, increase and control the quality of what we buy, eliminate the higher prices of institutional middle men, support local farmers by providing them with a direct urban market, encourage the rebirth of the American family farm and encourage organic farming methods in and outside of urban areas.

Public Transportation

It has been said that a transportation system is the lifeblood of a city or an economy. If we hope to revitalize African-American communities by consuming fewer resources and being highly efficient in what we do use, then we must pay close attention to our transportation system. We need to advocate for transit policies that support our local, regional and national sustainability efforts (35).

- African-Americans should support the policy of having a balanced transportation system that utilizes all types of vehicles and modes and is no longer overly dependent on automobiles. This would reduce automobile congestion, improve travel times, increase the efficiency of the cars and trucks that do remain in service, improve air quality and lower the incidence of respiratory disease. All of this would be beneficial to African-American communities given that we suffer disproportionately from the negative impacts of automobile use and would contribute to lowering our health care costs.
- In determining a new mix of transportation modes, we must shift more of our ridership from cars/trucks to

public transportation. It is a well-known fact that the cost per passenger-mile is extremely high for automobiles and far lower for public transportation, especially rail transportation. This would help to reduce the percentage of consumer spending devoted to transportation costs; a critical need in African-American communities. While this does not call for the total elimination of cars and trucks it does mean reducing their role in our system.

- We need to advocate for the expansion of public transportation systems in order to make it more convenient for shoppers, senior citizens and disabled riders. The transit system must have convenient routes that provide excellent connectivity between places of employment, education, medical services, shopping and cultural amenities.

- This is essential for African-American communities that have low rates of automobile ownership and are transit-dependent.

- We should support the expansion of commuter rail service, provided there are two-way schedules throughout the day so that people from African-American communities can have a "reverse" commute and be able to access employment, recreation and shopping (where the prices are generally lower) outside of major urban areas.

- We should support initiatives that call for the development of high speed rail passenger service and expanded railroad freight service. Rail is the cheapest way of transporting people and cuts down the final price we must pay for various goods and products. This policy would be very beneficial to our overall strategy of lowering consumer prices.

- The expansion of our public transportation system will not only benefit our environment but provides construction jobs during expansion projects and permanent jobs for the maintenance, repair and operation of the system.

Sustainable Development and Jobs

Critics of the environmental movement have often stated that any substantial environmental policy would cost our economy jobs and at times the African-American community has been confronted with this choice; a clean environment but fewer jobs. However, nothing could be further from the truth. The environmental movement and the strategy of sustainable development will bring together a host of new technologies and industries that will provide numerous opportunities as they replace the technologies of the industrial revolution (36). As stated earlier some of those technologies and industries include; solar energy, hydrogen fuel cells, wind technology, tidal turbines, geothermal heat sources, organic farming, public transportation and recycling facilities. Each of these will have a number of critical needs that must be met in order for them to grow. Given the need for increased entrepreneurship and employment within African-American communities this is an excellent opportunity for African-Americans to get on the ground floor of a growing sector of the American economy. We must determine the role we wish to play in these emerging industries and the type of education required. The opportunities within these industries include;

- Owner/Investor
- Research and Development
- Manufacturing
- Senior Management
- Middle Management
- Entry-level employee
- Secondary and tertiary contracts for small businesses and suppliers
- Transportation
- Wholesale distribution
- Retail distribution
- Installation and repair

Conclusion

It is the our hope that through the pursuit of economic democracy, political empowerment, sustainable development and math/science literacy, African-American communities will overcome the poverty, unemployment, underdevelopment and dependency that has afflicted us for so long. The African-American experience has always played a central role in social movements aiming for fundamental change in America and so it will again in the 21st century.

We must seize upon the new knowledge and opportunities of this century to revitalize our communities, give hope to our people and reshape America. The hopes and dreams of our generation and those to come depend on what we choose to do now. If the problem of the 20th century was the problem of the color line, then let the 21st century be the century of our liberation.

Footnotes

1. WEB DuBois, The Souls of Black Folk, Chap.2, p.23
2. U.S. Statistical Abstract 2010, Table 229: Educational Attainment by Race and Hispanic Origin
3. Kenneth Clark, Dark Ghetto, Chap. 5
4. Federal Reserve Bank, Z1:Flow of Funds of the United States, 2010; Rutledge Capital Website, Nov.30, 2011 and John K. Scholz, and Kara Levine, U.S. Black-White Wealth Inequity: A Survey, June 9, 2003.
5. U.S. Bureau of Labor Statistics, 2010: Table 2100, Race of Reference person: Average Annual Expenditures and Characteristics, Consumer Expenditure Survey.
6. Wikipedia, List of Countries by Gross Domestic Product, October 2011
7. John Restakis, Humanizing the Economy, Introduction, p.3
8. The Coop Handbook Collective, The Food Co-op Handbook, Chap. 3, p.32-44
9. Wessels: Living History Farm, Farmer's Share of the Food Dollar, p.1-3
10. WEB Dubois, Dusk of Dawn, Chap.7 p.216
11. Gar Alperowitz, Rebuilding America, Chap. 9, p.162-164
12. U.S. Dept of Labor, Bureau of Labor Statistics, Union Members Summary for 1954
13. N.Y. Times, "Real Wages Fail to Match a Rise in Productivity", August 28, 2006
14. U.S. Dept. of Labor, Bureau of Labor Statistics, Union Members Survey for 2010

15. Phillip Foner, Organized Labor and the Black Worker, Chap.26, p.425
16. William K. Tabb (editor), Sunbelt/Snowbelt, Chapter 6, Capital Mobility Versus Upward Mobility: The Racially Discriminatory Consequences of Plant closings and Corporate Relocations, p.152-162, Gregory Squires
17. Manning Marable *et al*, How Capitalism Underdeveloped Black America, The Crisis of the Black Working Class, Chap.1, p.23-52
18. Manning Marable, Race and Labor Matters in the New U.S. Economy, Part 1, Chap.1, P.17-26
19. Antonio Gramsci: Selected Political Writings, 1910-1920, Unions and Councils, Part II, Chap. 25, p.98-102
20. C.B. McPherson, Democratic Theory Part I, Chap.6, p. 120-142
21. Jeff Gates, The Ownership Solution, Chap.5, p.50-67
22. Jeff Gates, The ownership Solution, Chap. 6, p. 68-78
23. For information on land trusts please the websites for the Institute for Community Economics and the Dudley Street Neighborhood Initiative
24. See the website for La Nuestra Communidad Development Corp., Overview and Mission Statement
25. Gregory Squires, Capital and Communities in Black and White, Chap.4, p.65-90
26. Michael Parenti, Democracy for The Few, Chap.11, p.184-204
27. Norman Birnbaum, The Crisis of Industrial Society, Chap. 2, p.58-74
28. Cynthia Hamilton, Taylorism and Industrial Organization, PHD Dissertation, 1981
29. Barry Commoner, The Poverty of Power, Chap.7, p.145-197
30. E.F. Schumacher, Small is Beautiful, Chap. 2, p.171-190
31. Hazel Henderson, The Politics of the Solar Age, Chap. 6, p.128-154
32. United Church of Christ, Toxic Waste and Race
33. See the Website for the PRED property management consulting firm

34. Barry Commoner, The Poverty of Power, Chap.6, p.113-144
35. See the website for ON THE MOVE, Statement of Principles, 2002
36. Van Jones, The Green-Collar Economy, Chap.5, p.114-144
37. Paul Hawkin, The Next Economy, Chap.1, p.6-27
38. Robert Hazen & James Trefil, Science matters; Achieving Scientific Literacy, Introduction, p. xi-xiv
39. GAO Report, Science, Technology, Engineering and Mathematics Trends and the Role of Federal Programs, 2006
40. See the ACT website, ACT STEM Policy Report, 2006
41. See Wikipedia List of Countries by Steel Production; See The Top Five of Everything website-Top Five Shipbuilding Countries
42. Thomas Friedman, The World Is Flat, Chap.7, p. 266-267

Bibliography

Works Cited

1. Gar Alperowitz and Jeff Faux, *Rebuilding America: A Blueprint for the New Economy*, Pantheon Books, New York, 1984
2. Norman Birnbaum, *The Crisis of Industrial Economy*, Oxford University Press, Oxford, 1969
3. Kenneth Clark, *Dark Ghetto*, 1960
4. Barry Commoner, *The Poverty of Power: Energy and the Economic Crisis*, Alfred A. Knopf Inc., New York, 1976
5. W.E.B. DuBois, *The Souls of Black Folk*, Fawcett Publications, New York, 1961
6. W.E.B. DuBois, *Dusk of Dawn: An Essay Toward An Autobiography of a Race Concept*, First Schocken Edition, New York, 1968
7. Philip Foner, Organized Labor and the Black Worker 1619-1973, International publishers, New York, 1974
8. The Food Co-op Collective, *The Food Co-op Handbook*, Houghton Mifflin Co. Boston, 1975
9. Thomas Friedman, *The World Is Flat: A Brief History of the Twenty-First Century,* Farrar, Straus, and Giroux, New York, 2005
10. Jeff Gates, *The Ownership Solution: Toward a Shared Capitalism for the 21st Century*, Addison-Wesley, Reading, Mass., 1998
11. Antonio Gramsci, *Selections from Political Writings 1910-1920*, International Publishers, New York, 1977

12. Paul Hawkin, *The Next Economy*, Ballentine Books, New York, 1983

13. Robert Hazen & James Trefil, *Science Matters: Achieving Scientific Literacy*, Anchor Books/Doubleday, New York, 1991

14. Hazel Henderson, *The Politics of the Solar Age: Alternatives to Economics*, Anchor Press/Doubleday, Garden City, New York, 1981

15. Van Jones, *The Green Collar Economy: How One Solution Can Fix Our Two Biggest Problems*, Harper One, New York, 2008

16. Manning Marable, *How Capitalism Underdeveloped Black America*, South End Press, Boston, 1983

17. Manning Marable, Immanuel Ness and Joseph Wilson, *Race and Labor Matters in the New U.S. Economy*, Rowman & Littlefield Publishers, Inc., New York, 2006

18. C.B. MacPherson, *Democratic Theory*: Essays in Retrieval, Clarendon Press, Oxford, 1973

19. Michael Parenti, *Democracy For The Few*, St. Martin's Press, New York, 1980

20. John Restakis, *Humanizing the Economy: Coopertives in the Age of Capital*, New Society Publishers, Canada, 2010

21. Larry Sawers & William K. Tabb, *Sunbelt/Snowbelt: Urban Development and Regional Restructuring*, Oxford University Press, Oxford, 1984

22. E.F. Schumacher, *Small Is Beautiful: Economics As If People Mattered*, Perennial Library/Harper & Row, New York, 1975

23. Gregory Squires, *Capital and Communities In Black And White: The Intersections of Race, Class, and Uneven Development*, State University of New York Press, 1994

Articles

N.Y. Times, "Real Wages Fail to Match a Rise in Productivity", August 28, 2006

Dissertations

Cynthia Hamilton, **Taylorism and Industrial Organization**, PHD dissertation, Boston University, 1981

Government Documents

GAO Report, Testimony before the Committee on Education and the Workforce, House of Representatives: **Science, Technology, Engineering and Mathematics Trends and the Role of Federal Programs**, Statement of Cornelia M. Ashby, Director, Education, Workforce and Income Security Issues, May 2006

U.S. Bureau of Labor Statistics, Table 2100, **Race of Reference Person: Average Annual Expenditures and Characteristics, Consumer Expenditure Survey**, 2010

U.S. Dept. of Labor, Bureau of Labor Statistics, **Union Members Survey**, 2010

U.S. Statistical Abstract, Table 229, **Educational Attainment by Race and Hispanic Origin**, 2010

Federal Reserve Bank Z1: **Flow of Funds of the United States**, 2010

Reports

John K. Scholz, and Kara Levine, U.S. Black-White Wealth Inequity: A Survey, June 9, 003

United Church of Christ, Toxic Waste and Race, 1985 and 2007

Websites

ACT: ACT-Stem Policy Report, 2006

Dudley Street Neighborhood Initiative

Institute for Community Economics

La Nuestra Communidad

ON THE Move: Greater Boston Transportation Justice Coalition

PRED: Property Management Consulting Firm

Rutledge Capital

Top Five of Everything

Wessels: Living History Farm, Farmer's Share of the Food Dollar

Wikipedia, List of Countries by Gross Domestic Product

Wikipedia, List of countries by Steel Production

www.ingramcontent.com/pod-product-compliance
Lightning Source LLC
Chambersburg PA
CBHW030539290526
45786CB00004B/1784